# North American Animals

by Dawne Allette

illustrated by Alan Baker

Tamarind

Welcome to America.
This land is our home.

We will show you the animals,
where they play and where they roam.

**Armadillo** burrows
in the Texas sun.

**Bison** and

**black bear**
are going for a run.

**Coyotes** are prowling in the wild, wild West.

**Deer** are looking for a place to rest.

**Eagle** hunts in the afternoon light.

**Ferret**

comes awake
only at night.

# Gila monster

stores fat in its tail.

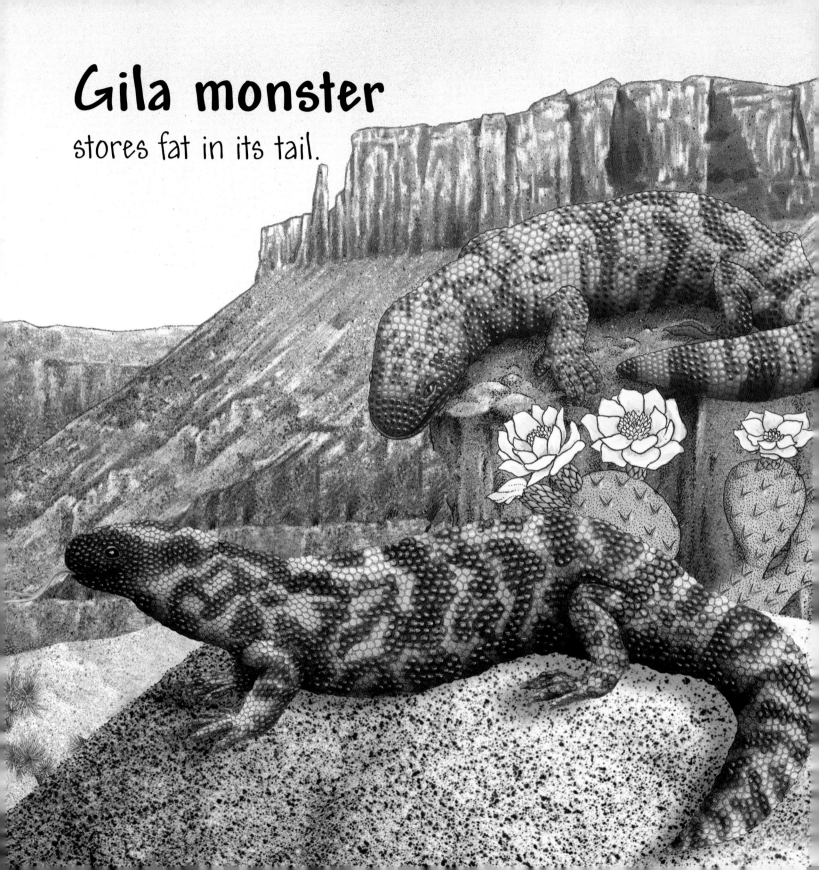

**Harp seal** is hunted
by the killer whale.

**Ibis** lives in wetlands

and is a wading bird.

**Javelinas** like to travel together in a herd.

**Kingsnake** helps us to be rid of rats.

Lynx

is one
of
the endangered
cats.

On the high plains, **mustangs** run loose.

**Nene** is a rare Hawaiian goose.

**Otters** swim like fish but they don't have gills.

Did you know **porcupines** can have 30,000 quills?

# Queen conch is a sea snail that makes its own shell.

**Raccoon**
is a mammal that
knows the city well.

**Skunk** squirts a liquid that smells like rotten eggs.

**Tarantula**

has eight eyes
and

very
hairy
legs.

**Utah prairie dogs** live
in burrows in the ground.

# Virginia opossums play dead making no sound.

You smell him, then you see him...

It's **wolverine**.

**Xenops** lives in tree holes and is not often seen.

See that **yellow jacket?**

He has quite a sting.

Last but not least
is the **zebra long wing**.

# North American animals

North America is a huge continent that stretches from the frozen open spaces of Canada, through the mountains, plains and deserts of the United States, to the hot tropical forests of Mexico.

**Armadillo** – a small mammal with a hard shell. It lives alone and comes out at night to hunt. It is a very good digger and uses its sharp claws to find grubs and insects to eat, as well as to dig its burrow.

**Bison** (commonly called buffalo in the US) – a large, shaggy-haired grass-eating mammal, like a huge cow. Herds of bison used to roam across the American plains. They were almost hunted to extinction in the 19th century by the Europeans who settled in America.

**Black bear** – a bear that lives all across America. It has a shuffling walk because it has flat feet and its back legs are longer than its front legs.

**Coyote** – a wild dog found all over North America. Coyotes live in packs but usually hunt in pairs. They are hunted by humans, so they now only come out at night.

**Deer** (**Mule**) – a deer with big ears like a donkey or mule (which is how it got its name). This deer does not run, but moves in leaps and bounds with all four feet coming down at the same time.

**Eagle** (**Bald**) – a large bird of prey that is the national symbol of the United States. It lives near water and hunts by swooping down and snatching fish straight out of the water with its talons. It holds the fish in one claw and tears at its flesh with the other. It is called Bald eagle from piebald, a word that describes an animal with large patches of white on its body. The eagle has a white head and white tail feathers.

**Ferret** (**American black-footed**) – a small meat-eating mammal, in the same family as weasels and otters. It feeds mostly on prairie dogs. But it also hunts small mammals, birds and even insects. It is a protected animal as it is almost extinct.

**Gila monster** – a large poisonous lizard with scaly skin. It eats bird and reptile eggs that it can smell from far away. It can also crush small birds and frogs and swallow them whole. In the desert, where it lives, there is often little food. At these times, it can exist on the fat stored in its tail. It is too heavy and slow to be dangerous to humans.

**Harp seal** – a sea mammal that lives in icy waters. Females come onto the ice pack to give birth to one pup each year. The pup cannot swim until it is about a month old. The seal is hunted by the Killer whale or Orca, a fierce, meat-eating dolphin.

**Ibis** (**American white**) – a large bird that pokes its beak into the mud to catch small fish, shrimp and shellfish. It lives in hot, tropical marshlands in the south of the United States and Mexico.

**Javelina** (or **Peccary**) – a small mammal that looks like a pig and is part of the same family as pigs and hippos. It has short, straight tusks that it uses for crushing seeds and cutting the roots of the plants that it eats. It can rub its tusks together to make a chattering noise to warn off predators.

**Kingsnake (Scarlet)** – a small snake found only in Florida. Its pattern copies that of the poisonous coral snake. This protects it from attack. Predators keep away because they think the snake is dangerous. It eat rats, lizards, birds and eggs and even eats other snakes.

**Lynx (Canadian)** – a big wild cat, almost twice the size of a pet cat. It lives alone in the coldest parts of the continent. It comes out at night to hunt hares, small rodents and sometimes even deer.

**Mustang** – a wild horse. Long ago there were no horses in America. European settlers brought the first ones. Some strays managed to survive away from humans and so the first herds of wild horses came into existence.

**Nene** (or **Hawaiian goose**) – the rarest goose in the world which is only found on the islands of Hawaii.

**Otter** – a fish-eating mammal that lives in rivers and along the sea shore. It has webbed feet that help it to move easily through the water.

**Porcupine** – a rodent (like a rat or beaver) with sharp spines all over its body. It is only distantly related to hedgehogs. It is an excellent climber and spends much of its life up in the trees.

**Queen conch** – a kind of large sea snail that makes its own shell. The shell is a beautiful spiral shape with a flared lip that is often a deep coral pink colour. This snail lives in the hot Caribbean Sea and feeds on plant matter.

**Raccoon** – a mammal that is seen around houses all over America. It eats anything, from berries and fruit to chickens and small mammals. It used to live in the forest, but discovered there is plenty of food in towns and cities. It uses its front paws like hands and can easily open rubbish bins to steal food. It will even eat dog food!

**Skunk (Striped)** – a small mammal that only exists in America. There are many different kinds of skunk. They can all spray a smelly mist on any animal that threatens them. This puts predators off, so they leave the skunk alone. At dawn and dusk, it comes out to hunt mice and search for eggs and dead meat.

**Tarantula (California)** – a large, hairy spider that is very common in the United States. It lives in hot desert areas. It builds a large web but does not wait for prey to get trapped in it. The tarantula leaves its web to hunt the small birds it feeds on. A tarantula can live for up to 30 years. It is poisonous to animals. To humans its bite feels like a bee sting, but some people may be allergic.

**Utah prairie dog** – a small, burrowing rodent in the same family as squirrels. There are many kinds of prairie dogs all over America. The Utah species is the most threatened and the smallest. It eats seeds, grasses and flowers. It lives in huge 'towns' under the ground, formed of linked tunnels and chambers.

**Virginia opossum** – a marsupial that carries its very young babies in a pouch on its belly (like kangaroos). This opossum was originally from South America but moved into North America many million years ago. Now it can be found all over the continent. It is about the size of a cat. It hunts at night and eats almost anything, from fruit to insects and small mammals. When an opossum feels in danger, it falls over and lies still, giving off a smelly liquid from its mouth so that it seems to be dead. That usually puts off any predator.

**Wolverine** – the largest member of the weasel family. It is very strong and has been known to hunt sick, old moose in winter! It has a special molar in the back of its mouth that is turned sideways. This allows the wolverine to tear off meat that is frozen solid and also to crush bones to extract the marrow. It is very shy so is rarely seen by people. It marks its territory with a smelly substance that can be smelled from far away!

**Xenops** – this small bird lives in the tropical forests of Mexico. To make a nest, it fills a hole in a rotten branch with shredded bits of plants. It feeds on insects.

**Yellow jacket** – a common name for a wasp in the United States. It lives in colonies, including workers, queens and males. It makes a nest out of chewed wood mixed with spit.

**Zebra longwing** – a striped butterfly that lives in the southern part of the United States and Mexico.

For Ellen Lowe with love
D.A.
To my brother Michael with love
A.B.

NORTH AMERICAN ANIMALS
TAMARIND BOOKS 978 1 848 53010 2

Published in Great Britain by Tamarind Books,
a division of Random House Children's Books
A Random House Group Company

This edition published 2009

1 3 5 7 9 10 8 6 4 2

Set in Andy

TAMARIND BOOKS
61–63 Uxbridge Road, London, W5 5SA

www.tamarindbooks.co.uk
www.kidsatrandomhouse.co.uk
www.rbooks.co.uk

Addresses for companies within The Random House Group Limited can be found at:
www.randomhouse.co.uk/offices.htm

THE RANDOM HOUSE GROUP Limited Reg. No. 954009

A CIP catalogue record for this book is available from the British Library.

Printed and bound in China